MW00901918

THE
RAPTORS
of
North
America

An Introduction to North American Birds of Prey

Doug Thal DVM

Copyright © Doug Thal DVM and Thal Enterprises 2024

All rights reserved. No part of this book may be reproduced or transmitted in any form or by any means, electronic or mechanical, including photocopying, recording, or by any information storage and retrieval system, without written permission from the author, except for the inclusion of brief quotations in a review.

ABOUT THE AUTHOR

MY STORY AND WHY I DID THIS.

I am an equine (horse) veterinarian, in private horse practice since 1993. What gives me the credibility to write a guide to raptors? Let me explain. I grew up on our family ranch in northern New Mexico, and I have been fascinated by raptors from as far back as I can remember. From the age of 5 years, I had a rare opportunity to be around many raptor species daily, and I just fell in love with the birds. All these years later, I still am.

On the ranch, Golden Eagles nested on the cliffs of the river canyon. Juvenile Bald Eagles visited our calving pasture in late winter, eating placentas from the newborn calves. Prairie Falcons chased ducks at the ponds, and Sharp-shinned and Cooper's Hawks grabbed blackbirds and starlings from the cattle feeders at our corrals. Red-Tailed Hawks and Great Horned Owls nested in the big cottonwood trees around our house at headquarters.

Of all raptors, I have always been most captivated by the regal Golden Eagle. For generations, there's been a nesting pair in the Coyote River canyon (we call it The Gap), in the middle of a sheer orange sandstone cliff. I spent much of my early childhood watching those birds at their nest, along with many other species, from my rock blind on the opposite side of the canyon. I was fortunate enough to witness rarely-documented, amazing eagle behaviors over the years.

I have always been outspoken in my defense of raptors, especially Golden Eagles. In about 1977, at the age of 10 years, I wrote a letter to the editor of an agricultural newspaper- the West Texas Livestock Weekly- condemning their articles that supported mass killing of Golden Eagles as a response to lamb losses experienced by ranchers. Instead, I suggested that "better livestock management" might help prevent losses. I created quite a stir in the industry, especially for a 10 year old! My mother was very involved in the livestock industry through those years, and she had ranchers from the whole region asking her to keep control of her son! Interestingly though, she also had a progressive few commend me for trying to suggest a better way.

I was also fascinated by falconry as a child. In the mid-1970's, at age 10, I was able to get a state wildlife rehabilitation license, and I rehabilitated about 20 raptors over about a 4-year period before my teen years, when I became too distracted by working on the ranch- and by adolescence- to continue the work. I learned basic falconry techniques for handling the birds. My mentor was a retired orthopedic surgeon who lived near Santa Fe, Phil Schultz. Phil was a falconer, and at that time, the leading rehabilitator of raptors in the region. He was kind enough to teach me about handling raptors and caring for them, and I will be forever grateful to him for that.

I also have always been interested in raptor identification. In 1980, when I was 14, I created "An Algorithmic System for the Identification of New Mexican Hawks." The posters shown below were part of it, and I also created a computer program that asked the user a series of questions about the bird they had seen and returned an identification. It was all pretty crude, but for those days, kind of unique. The program was created in "BASIC," one of the early computer programming languages.

A word about the images...While some of these images are from photos my son and I have taken, it's important to know that one reason I was able to create this book relates to artificial intelligence (AI). I was able to make many of these images using AI, and given that I have some raptor knowledge, ensure that the images are fairly accurate. If I could not get AI to generate a good image, I modified the image until it was passable. I could not have done this without that new technology. I simply would not have had the time.

Other images are from stock photos, because I could not get AI to generate an image even close to reality. As of the time of this writing, generative AI is early in its public use, and it will sometimes create bizarre and inaccurate images—birds with 6 toes and 3 wings! Please beware of this if you use AI to create wildlife images! I have vetted these images and modified them. Here and there, though, there may be an inaccurate detail. Some of these species I have known all my life, while some I have never seen. It's been a bit of an experiment. Please do reach out and let me know if you find an inaccuracy.

In this simple guide, I briefly touch on 34 species of diurnal (day-active) raptors that are found in North America. It's only meant to be an introduction. It doesn't include "accidentals"- raptor species that occasionally show up in North America by accident, maybe lost, or blown off course. This is the kind of guide that can live in your car for quick reference, or could be an introductory book for kids. It's also intended to be a visual and informational reference for **"The Raptors of North America-A Coloring Book of North American Birds of Prey"**, a second volume. Learning to identify raptors takes time and experience. There is a lifetime of learning that can be done on the biology and life history of these birds. At the end of the book, I have listed some excellent learning resources for more detailed information on the biology and identification of the birds.

Today, there are many threats to these priceless creatures, here in North America and around the world. The most profound of these are habitat loss and climate change. Poisoning is also a huge problem for large raptors-, especially vultures- in Eurasia and Africa. Misinformed livestock producers still vilify vultures for killing their livestock, often without reason, and shoot or poison them. Just because vultures or eagles are consuming a dead calf does not mean they killed it.

Lead-bullet contamination of carcasses is another important and preventable cause of death for eagles, vultures, and condors in the US and many other large raptor species abroad. Lead was a major cause of the near extinction of the California Condor, and it is still hampering their recovery. I do some hunting myself, so I recognize hunters' need for functional ammunition, but its time to outlaw lead bullets. Copper ammunition is now widely available and works fine for all hunting applications. Please support lead ammunition bans in your state, and if you are a hunter, find a copper ammunition that works for you!

At the end of the book, I list some resources regarding lead's impact on raptors worldwide, a link to an article I wrote, and and some organizations working on solving this very solvable problem. I also list some organizations involved in raptor conservation.

While the concept of wind energy from turbines is a good one from the standpoint of reducing greenhouse gas production, wind turbines are bad for birds. As we speak, hundreds of thousands of acres of southwestern land (inhabited by raptors) are being developed as wind farms. Many eagles and other raptors are killed by these wind turbines. Mechanisms and modifications need to be developed to make them bird-safe, and they need to be placed in locations that minimize raptor impact.

We still have the family ranch, and I still love and watch raptors. They have enriched my life so much, and I hope they do the same for you.

Doug Thal DVM DABVP
Santa Fe, New Mexico

This is me in 1976, at age 9, with one of my first birds, a female American Kestrel. In the background is the white picket fence that surrounded the 150 year old adobe house I was raised in. My older brother rebuilt the house and lives there now.

This was a young Swainson's Hawk I rehabilitated and released in 1978.

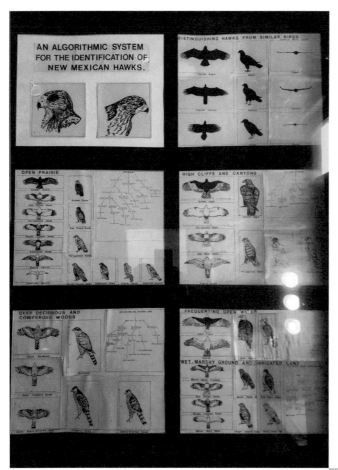

I have been interested in raptor identification for a long time. Here is a project I created when I was 14 years old, on the identification of New Mexican Raptors. It hangs in my son's bedroom.

I learned some watercolor in 2006 when I was injured and not able to work, and this Goshawk was one of my first paintings.

I found this lead-poisoned Golden Eagle on the ground near our eagle's nest on Thanksgiving Day of 2017. It later died. I had no idea what a huge problem lead was for these birds, until I did some research.

This poor Osprey became tangled in fishing line and died hanging from a tree near a popular fishing spot in New Mexico. So much loss could be prevented if we all just did our part. Just pick up and dispose of your used fishing line!

Looking down on one of the eagle nest cliffs from the hillside above.

Golden Eagle country! The view northeast from above the eagle's nest

Looking south toward ranch headquarters from the walk to eagle's nest.

The "Gap" in fall- the Coyote River Canyon cliffs where the Golden Eagles nest.

TABLE OF CONTENTS

INTRODUCTION: WHAT IS A RAPTOR?

Few creatures command awe and admiration like raptors do. The word "raptor" actually comes from the Latin word "rapere" which means "to seize violently and take away". Sounds bad, but that is what these birds do. Also known as birds of prey, these are birds that have evolved to kill and eat other animals (in the case of eagles, hawks, falcons, kites and caracaras) or scavenge(in the case of vultures).

Many other birds eat insects and fish, but none of these are considered raptors. What then defines a raptor? A hooked bill and highly evolved killing feet are two features that tend to separate raptors from non-raptors. This book is about the diurnal (day-active) raptors of North America. Owls are not included here, but are considered nocturnal raptors.

Diurnal raptors belong to two primary taxonomic orders: the Accipitriformes (hawks, eagles, kites and Old World vultures) and Falconiformes (falcons and caracaras). A third. small order is Cathartiformes, which contains the New World (American) vultures, relatively more closely related to Acciptriformes.

A real surprise is that Acciptriformes and Falconiformes are not at all closely related. Falcons are actually more closely related to parrots and sparrows than they are to hawks and eagles! Why then do they look so generally similar? This is a great example of "evolutionary convergence". Over tens of millions of years, relatively unrelated groups tend to develop similar features to fill similar ecological niches. In plain terms, a "niche" is a particular environment and its opportunities and limitations.

Around the world, raptors are critical apex predators, and they have vital influence on their ecosystems. Their role as regulators of prey populations helps maintain ecological balance. Many raptor species play a crucial role in controlling rodent populations. Overpopulation of rodents results in a cascade of consequences to agriculture, and can also result in increased human disease.

Throughout world history, raptors have had spiritual significance to cultures around the globe, embodying strength and divine connection. Many Native American traditions have viewed- and continue to view- eagles as messengers between humans and the spiritual realm. In Ancient Egypt, the important god Horus was represented as a falcon, and was a symbol of the sky, the sun, and kingship. These are just two examples of raptors' universal symbolism of power and transcendence; there are hundreds more.

Falconry, the art of training raptors to hunt, has been a prestigious and noble tradition practiced for over 4000 years by many cultures worldwide. Originating in the far east, it spread to Europe and the middle east, symbolizing status and functioning as a means to procure food. Falconry is one more factor deeply connecting humans and these birds.

Despite their ecological importance and humanity's strong connection to the birds, many raptor species are in trouble. Habitat loss, fragmentation, and degradation- from uncontrolled development- threaten nesting sites and hunting grounds essential for their survival. Pesticides and poisons- intended to kill other animals impacting agriculture- have had devastating effects on raptor populations, leading to reproductive failures and population declines around the world. Collisions with vehicles, wind turbines, and electrocution by contact with live power lines are just a few more risks in a world full of hazards.

Humanity is now the steward of our natural world, and now is the time for us to step up and take whatever steps are necessary to solve the causes of raptor decline, and thus safeguard their future. There are some wonderful conservation success stories that involve raptors (Peregrine Falcon and California Condor to name two) , but there are so many species in peril and so much work to do. Raptors and the habitats that support them are precious, fragile and irreplaceable. We all must do our part to help ensure that future generations will be able to enjoy watching these splendid creatures in the wild, as we have.

ORDER: ACCIPTRIFORMES
FAMILY: ACCIPTRIDAE

EAGLES, HAWKS, HARRIERS, KITES

Acciptridae is by far the largest family within the order Accipitriformes, and it comprises eagles, hawks, kites, harriers, and the Old World vultures. Members of this family are distributed worldwide and display a broad range of sizes, plumage patterns, and hunting strategies. Eagles tend to be large, powerful hunters, while hawks are smaller and widely varied in form and behavior, eating eat smaller birds and mammals. Kites are known for their graceful flight and scavenging habits, while harriers are characterized by their unique, low, buoyant flight over open habitats, preying on small mammals and birds. Old World vultures are large raptors that play a crucial role in scavenging, utilizing keen eyesight to locate carrion.

EAGLES

Think of an eagle as any species of bird of prey larger and more powerful than Buteo hawks, and that eats live prey. That's not a very scientific definition, but that is how the word "eagle" is used. Globally, there are 68 species of eagles, from multiple genera- some not closely related at all-and all of these are called eagles. Most eagle species are from Eurasia and Africa.

North America is home to only two eagle species from two very different genera. These are the Bald Eagle (a sea eagle) and the Golden Eagle (a "true" eagle) . These two species are roughly the same size, but that is where the similarities end.

The Bald Eagle, typical of sea eagles, is usually found near water. It eats fish, waterfowl and carrion.

The Golden Eagle is a symbol of wild country: the mountains, high chaparral and canyons. While they sometimes eat carrion, Golden Eagles are also tremendous hunters, capable of taking relatively large game at high speeds. My favorite bird in the world- I have seen them take Canada Geese and Great Blue Herons out of the air. I have seen kill jackrabbits at a flat-out run, tumbling end over end in the dirt with their prey. I once saw a Golden Eagle knock a Great Horned Owl out of the air, which happened to fly across the Coyote River Canyon at the wrong moment in the middle of the day.

GOLDEN EAGLE
(Aquila chryseatos)

Male Size: 26-33 in (66-84 cm), **Wingspan:** 6.0-7.5 ft (1.8-2.3 m)

Female Size: 29-36 in (74-91 cm), **Wingspan:** 6.5-7.8 ft (2-2.4 m)

Winter Range: Throughout North America, particularly in the western mountains and chaparral.

Summer Range: North America, especially western mountainous regions and open country

Diet: Medium-sized mammals such as rabbits and prairie dogs, and some larger mammals up to the size of foxes, young coyotes, young deer and Pronghorn, as well as birds including waterfowl. Golden Eagles at our ranch regularly hunt Canada Geese and ducks.

Field Marks: A large, dark-brown bird, much larger than any hawk. Flatter-winged and larger than Turkey Vultures, dark brown not black, without the silver primary feathers and two-tone wings of the Turkey Vulture. They have a much larger head and larger, wider wings. Young birds have solid white patches under the wing and a broad white tail band. Adults have bright gold hackle feathers on the nape of the head. They appear more stable in flight than Turkey Vultures, without the characteristic rocking and folding of the wings seen in those birds. Juvenile Bald Eagles have more plank-like wings, whereas Goldens have a more rounded-out rear outline of the wing. The adults are solid dark brown with golden accents, especially the bright-gold hackle feathers of the head, which can be seen even from quite a long distance. Their legs are feathered to the toes.

Interesting Facts

Golden Eagles are known for their incredible speed, power, and agility, particularly during hunting. They are one of the most widely distributed species of eagle, with races found on all continents except Antarctica and Australia (where they have a close relative, the Wedge-tailed Eagle).

An AI-generated image of an adult Golden Eagle perched on a rocky spire. I think this image really captures the spirit of the bird.

A modified AI-generated image of a Golden Eagle in flight in mountainous country. Also quite accurate I thought.

BALD EAGLE
(Haliaetus leucocephalus)

Male Size: 30-34 in (76-86 cm), **Wingspan:** 6.6-7.5 ft (2-2.3 m)

Female Size: 35-37 in (89-94 cm), **Wingspan:** 7.5-8 ft (2.3-2.4 m)

Winter Range: Throughout North America. In our area, we have many wintering Bald Eagles, who gather near water. The most I have seen together at once at a lake near our family ranch is 29 eagles

Summer Range: Throughout North America.. Interestingly, they now summer more commonly in our area too.

Diet: Fish, birds (primarily waterfowl and water birds), carrion

Field Marks: Adults are hard to mistake for anything else. They have a very dark brown body with a pure white head and tail.

Young birds are dark and mottled with varying patches of white. Each year, they develop increasing white on their head and tail. Juvenile birds can be distinguished from Golden Eagles by their larger heads and large, yellow beaks. Unlike Goldens, their legs are un-feathered. In flight, their neck and head seem larger, their wings are flat and plank-like, without as much contour to the rear of the wing as those of the Golden. The patches of white on the young Golden's wing tend to be much better- defined, and young Goldens have an obvious broad white tail band.

Interesting Fact

It's the national bird of the United States. They have made a resurgence in population in the last 40 years, especially since the outlawing of DDT.

Modified AI generated image of a Bald Eagle perched on a stump by a river. I thought this was very good and left the image "as-is".

Juvenile Bald Eagle, nearing maturity- maybe 4 years old and developing the classic white head and tail. AI-generated image.

ACCIPITERS

Accipiters, known as the "short-winged hawks," are recognized for their remarkable agility and speed, particularly in wooded areas where they typically hunt. Sometimes called "true hawks", their short wings and long tails are adaptations for maneuvering through dense cover. They are known to be bold, fast, and aggressive hunters, with the smaller two species specializing in hunting birds. Worldwide, there are approximately 50 species within the Accipiter genus. In North America, we have only three species, which I'll organize by size, from smallest to largest.

SHARP-SHINNED HAWK
(Accipiter striatus)

Male Size: 9.4-13.4 in (24-34 cm), **Wingspan:** 16.9-22.1 in (43-56 cm)

Female Size: 11.4-15.8 in(29-40cm), **Wingspan:** 22.4-26.8 in(57-68 cm)

Winter Range: Almost all of the United States, into Mexico and Central America

Summer Range: Southern Canada, and northern North America, extending into Alaska and Canada. Populations of permanent residents in the mountainous west and the northeast, and even down into Mexico and South America.

Diet: Small birds up to the size of blackbirds and starlings, and sometimes larger, often caught out of the air after a rapid pursuit. Occasional small mammals and insects.

Field Marks: The size of a large Robin. Very short, rounded wings, with a long, banded (squared off) tail. Like most Accipiters, it flies with a few rapid flaps and a fast glide, often close to the ground. It will whip into a flock of feeding sparrows and snatch one out of the air so quickly it can be hard for an observer to register what happened. It can also sometimes soar and circle high in the sky, especially during migration. The adult is slate blue on the back with rufous bars across the front. Juveniles are brown and white with brownish streaks. Markings are very similar to the Cooper's Hawk. The Cooper's head and neck protrude forward in front of the wing in flight, whereas the Sharp-shinned gives the appearance of a short neck and head positioned behind the line of the front of the wing. The "Sharpie" is significantly smaller than the Cooper's on average. There is overlap, though—a large female Sharp-shinned may be nearly as large as a small male Cooper's, and it can be hard to judge.

Interesting Facts

The Sharp-shinned Hawk is the smallest hawk in North America (the American Kestrel is a falcon). Its name comes from the keel on its legs, a ridge that happens to be "sharp." They are one of the most common raptors at hawk watch sites during migration.

Immature Sharp-shinned in flight. A classic Accipiter shape in flight, with short, rounded wings, and long squared-off tail. The young bird has a bright yellow eye. From istock (Supercaliphotolistic)

Adult Sharp-shinned Hawk. About the size of a robin, but not nearly as "nice". Notice the dark cap, which extends down the back of the neck, whereas the Cooper's cap is more limited to the top of the head. (Modified AI image.)

COOPER'S HAWK
(Accipiter cooperi)

Male Size: 14.6-15.3in (37-39 cm), **Wingspan:** 24.4-35.4 in (62-90 cm)

Female Size: 16.5-17.7in (42-45cm), **Wingspan:** 29.5-35.4in (75-90 cm)

Winter Range: Forested habitat throughout the United States. Some migrate into Mexico and Central America in winter.

Summer Range: Forested habitat, including urban ones, through North America and southern Canada

Diet: Birds up to the size of crows, more rarely small mammals

Field Marks: A little larger than a large Robin, up to crow-sized, with short rounded wings and a very long, banded tail. The average Cooper's Hawk is significantly larger than the average Sharp-shinned. There is overlap, though —a large female Sharp-shinned may be nearly as large as a small male Cooper's. So its important to find other ways of differentiating. Flies with a few flaps and a glide (but a little slower flapping than the Sharpie), often close to the ground, but sometimes flaps and circles high too.

Markings are very similar to the Sharp-shinned. The adult is slate-blue on the back with rufous bars across the front.The dark cap on the head of the adult Cooper's is limited to the head whereas it goes down the neck in the Sharp-shinned. Juveniles have a brown back and light belly with brownish streaks. The Cooper's head and neck protrude forward in front of the wing in flight, whereas the Sharp-shinned gives the appearance of a short neck and head positioned behind the line of the front of the wing.

Interesting Fact

Cooper's Hawks have adapted well to urban environments. Some suburban areas actually have the highest population density of the bird in North America. This is one species that has found opportunity and success in the Anthropocene era!

Cooper's adult- coloration is very similar to the adult Sharp-shinned. It's the same shape, but larger. One difference is that the dark cap is more limited to the head and doesn't extend down the neck as obviously as the Sharpie's. (AI modified)

Cooper's Hawk adult. Orange-barred breast. Long, narrow, banded tail. From an istock photo (Steve Samples)

Cooper's Hawk immature in flight. Long, narrow, banded tail. Streaked breast, note that the head extends beyond leading edge of wing. The tail is more rounded than that of the Sharpie. (From an istock photo – Wichyanan L.)

AMERICAN GOSHAWK
(Accipiter gentilis)

Male Size: 17.7-20.9 in (45-53 cm), **Wingspan:** 40.5-46.1 in (103-117 cm)

Female Size: 20.5-24.8 in (52-63 cm), **Wingspan:** 40.9-46.5 in (104-118 cm)

Winter Range: Northern United States, through the mountainous, forested west, and down into the high Sierra Madres in Mexico. In general, it is more rare in the southern states.

Summer Range: North America, extends further into Alaska and Canada.

Diet: Birds up to the size of crows, geese, and ducks, mammals like rabbits and squirrels

Field Marks: A large bird, as long as a Red-tailed Hawk and larger than crows. The adult is dark gray with a lighter belly and fine gray barring, with prominent white eyebrows. The juvenile is brown with a lighter belly with vertical brown streaks, but still with some white on the eyebrow. The Goshawk is of the same general build as its smaller cousins, the Cooper's Hawk and Sharp-shinned Hawk, and moves similarly but more powerfully. It typically makes several flaps and a fast glide, usually low to the ground, and then swoops up into the low branches of a tree. It tends to be more secretive than those birds, found in deeper, more undisturbed forests, and so they are much more rarely seen.

Interesting Facts

The American Goshawk is a powerful and aggressive hunter, and it is the largest and most robust of the three species in the Accipiter genus in North America. It was called the Northern Goshawk until recently.

An adult Goshawk lands on a post. .Note the long, banded tail, fine barring on breast, and white above eye. Image modified from istock photo (ian600f)

Adult American Goshawk- red eye and white stripe on brow. (AI generated and modified to make accurate.)

BUTEOS

Buteo is the genus of "fan-tailed soaring hawks". These tend to be relatively heavy-bodied, broad-winged, medium to large-sized raptors. The genus Buteo has nearly 30 species, found over the Americas, Europe, Asia and Africa. This genus is called "buzzards" in other parts of the world, not to be confused with the American slang expression "buzzard" which usually refers to Turkey Vultures. Many of our North American Buteo species have dark and light morphs (color variations), making it hard to identify them by color alone. I won't go into that here, as you can find those color morphs in more advanced guides, but be on the lookout for these variations. It made sense to organize 9 North American Buteo species by size, starting with the largest this time.

FERRUGINOUS HAWK
(Buteo regalis)

Male Size: 20-23 in (51-58 cm), **Wingspan:** 53-56 in (135-142 cm)
Female Size: 23-27 in (58-69 cm), **Wingspan:** 56-60 in (142-152 cm)
Winter Range: Western United States,
Summer Range: Prairies, chapparal and rangeland of the western interior of North America and into Canada. The great plains.
Diet: Rodents, especially ground squirrels, gophers and prairie dogs and rabbits.
Field Marks- Generally the Ferruginous is a very light-colored and large, long-winged Buteo, with a light-colored head. Close up, the mouth is large, extending past the level of eye. Wings and tail are obviously longer and relatively more narrow than those of Red-tail, and the wings are held in a shallow "V" (called a dihedral) when viewed from the front. The adult has rusty-colored legs and shoulders. In flight, the dark, rust-colored legs form a noticeable dark "V"on an otherwise pale bird. Like the Rough-Leg, the legs are feathered to the toes.

Interesting Facts

It's the largest of the Buteo hawks in North America and has a spectacular pale and rusty plumage. The name "Ferruginous" refers to the rust color of the legs and back. A very large mouth is an adaptation for eating rodents like pocket gophers whole.

Ferruginous Hawk up close. Note the really wide mouth. This was modified from an image I found on istock.

A Ferruginous in flight. I had to really modify this AI-generated image. Note the dark legs and very light body and head.

Ferruginous Hawk sitting on a post- dark feathered legs, large mouth, pale bird with rufous shoulders and legs. From unsplash image (David Thielen)

ROUGH-LEGGED HAWK
(Buteo lagopus)

Male Size: 18-20 in (46-51 cm), **Wingspan:** 52-54 in (132-137 cm)

Female Size: 20-24 in (51-61 cm), **Wingspan:** 54-60 in (137-152 cm)

Winter Range: Throughout the United States except for the south-eastern states

Summer Range: Northern Canada and Alaska. Nests in the Arctic, not in the lower 48 states.

Diet: Small mammals, particularly lemmings and voles.

Field Marks– Longer and narrower-winged than Red-tailed Hawk, with a smaller head and beak. The head is usually light-colored, with dark lower belly and dark "wrists" on wings and with an obvious white tail band. Smaller head and beak than Ferruginous and slimmer body than Red Tail. This bird hovers far more than the other Buteo hawks.

Interesting Fact

The name "Rough-legged" comes from the fact that the legs are feathered down to the toes, an adaptation for cold Arctic environments.

Light-phase Rough-Legged Hawk-note the dark "wrists", lower breast, and axilla (arm pits) White and black banded tail. Heavily-modified AI photo.

Adult Rough-Legged Hawk perched in a tree. Note the small and pale head, and small bill, and the dark lower breast. Modified from an istock photo (Jeff Edwards).

The back of a Rough-Legged Hawk- small, light-colored head, and white tail band. Grays and darks. From an istock photo.

RED TAILED HAWK
(Buteo jamaicensis)

Male Size: 18-22 in (45-56 cm), **Wingspan:** 45-52 in (114-133 cm)
Female Size: 20-26 in (50-65 cm), **Wingspan:** 52-56 in (133-142 cm)
Winter Range: Common throughout North America
Summer Range: Common throughout North America
Diet: Small mammals, birds, reptiles
Field Marks-A very common, large and stocky Buteo often perched conspicuously on power poles along roads. Light belly and dark head and back. Reddish-orange tail in adults. Younger birds have pale-brownish, lightly-banded tail. In flight, it has broad wings and fan-shaped reddish tail (adult). Multiple flaps and glides, and circles on updrafts, soars, and very rarely hovers. There are multiple color morphs (phases), from very dark (called Harlan's) to very light (called Krider's). This makes differentiating these from other similarly colored Buteos a challenge.

Interesting Facts

Adult birds are known for their distinctive reddish-orange tail, especially visible in flight. This is by far the most common large raptor in North America. It is highly adaptable to almost any environment, including even large and busy cities. Their shrill, harsh scream is the classic hawk or eagle sound heard in just about every western film!

An adult Red-tail in flight. modified from an unsplash photo (Joshua J Cotten).

From an AI – generated image – an adult Red-tailed Hawk. Stocky, large Buteo with, with dark brown head, light chest, dark back and red tail.

From an AI – generated image – an adult Red-tailed Hawk. Dark brown head, light chest, dark back and red tail. Bare yellow legs.

ZONE-TAILED HAWK
(Buteo albonotatus)

Male Size: 17-19 in (43-48 cm), **Wingspan:** 47-55 in (120-140 cm)
Female Size: 19-22 in (48-56 cm), **Wingspan:** 50-57 in (127-145 cm)
Winter Range: Central and South America
Summer Range: Southwestern United States to South America
Diet: Small mammals, birds, reptiles
Field marks– Their coloration is very similar to that of Turkey Vultures with dark body and head, dark wing lining and silvery wing feathers, and they have relatively long, narrow wings. Black and white banded tail. Somewhat smaller than the Turkey Vultures it is often seen with.

Interesting Facts

They often soar with vultures, probably using this association to surprise prey. This is an important adaptation for these birds. This is also how birders find Zone-tails. They just look for groups of Turkey Vultures and find one that looks a little different.

Zone-tailed hawk- note the 2 tone long wings very similar to Turkey Vulture at first glance. But with a single white tail band. Modified AI image.

Zone Tailed Hawk- modified from istock image.

SWAINSON'S HAWK
(Buteo swainsoni)

Male Size: 17-20 in (48-56 cm), **Wingspan:** 48-52 in (122-137 cm)
Female Size: 19-22 in (56-64 cm), **Wingspan:** 48-53 in (132-147 cm)
Winter Range: South America
Summer Range: Western North America
Diet: Insects, especially grasshoppers, smaller mammals than Red-tail eats. Not as powerful or aggressive a bird as the Red-tail.
Field Marks- Look for these birds only in summer into early fall. Swainson's is smaller and much more slim than the Red-tail. They have relatively longer and narrower wings, and flap more than Red-tails. Adult bird has dark head with white near bill, and dark upper chest. The pattern of contrasting white wing linings and darker flight feathers is a classic field mark used to identify this bird in flight, from a distance.

Interesting Facts

Known for one of the longest migrations of any American raptor, traveling from North America as far south as Argentina and back each year. I raised several young Swainson's Hawks when I was about 12 years old. One became extremely bonded to me- she would follow me on the tractor when I was baling hay, and would pick up voles from the field. In the fall before she left on migration, she would even follow my vehicle part way to school!

Swainson's Hawk adult in flight. Note the dark upper breast, white around the beak, white "wing linings"- leading edge of wings. This is an important field mark. Image modified from AI generated image.

An adult Swainson's Hawk adult sitting on a post. . Note the brown band across the upper chest. Modified from istock photo.

SHORT-TAILED HAWK
(Buteo brachyurus)

Male Size: 16-18 in (41-46 cm), **Wingspan:** 33-35 in (84-89 cm)
Female Size: 17-19 in (43-48 cm), **Wingspan:** 35-37 in (89-94 cm)
Winter Range: Woodlands of most of Florida, Mexico, and widespread in Central and South America
Summer Range: Woodlands of only southern Florida, Mexico and south.
Diet: Mostly a bird specialist, but also small mammals
Field Marks- A small to medium-sized Buteo found mostly in wooded areas. It has a very small range in the US. It is similar to Broad-Winged in appearance, but longer-winged. Light phases are very white breasted in sharp contrast with dark head. White wing linings seen from below.

Interesting Fact

They are adept at maneuvering through dense forests and are often seen soaring high in the sky above forests. I have never seen this bird.

Short-tailed Hawk in flight. Note sharp contrast between dark head and light body and wings. It's tail really isn't that short! modified from AI image,

Short-tailed hawk perched. Modified from AI-generated image.

BROAD-WINGED HAWK
(Buteo platypterus)

Male Size: 13-17 in (34-43 cm), **Wingspan:** 31-37 in (79-94 cm)
Female Size: 14-18 in (36-46 cm), **Wingspan:** 32-39 in (81-99 cm)
Winter Range: Central and South America. Occasionally seen in southern Florida.
Summer Range: All of eastern North America
Diet: Small mammals, insects, amphibians
Field Marks: These are the smallest of the Buteo hawks in North America. Significantly smaller than the larger Buteos, even smaller than a crow. Tends to perch in forested areas and hunt from a perch. Adults have a prominent single white tail band.

Interesting Fact

This is a very common hawk in the eastern United States. They migrate in large groups, which can number in the thousands. These flocks are called "kettles".

Broad-winged hawk in flight. Note black and white banded tail. Modified from AI image,

Broad-winged hawk. Image modified from an unsplash photo (Naveen Naidu)

RED-SHOULDERED HAWK
(Buteo lineatus)

Male Size: 17-19 in (43-48 cm), **Wingspan:** 37-43 in (94-109 cm)

Female Size: 19-24 in (48-61 cm), **Wingspan:** 42-48 in (107-127 cm)

Winter Range: Forest and riparian zones in eastern states and near the Pacific coast

Summer Range: Same: eastern United States, coastal California

Diet: Small mammals, amphibians, reptiles, birds

Field Marks: A noisy, medium sized raptor with reddish shoulders and bold, white and black banded tail. There are multiple color variants in the different parts of the range.

Interesting Fact

They are noisy birds, often located by listening for their distinctive call.

Red-shouldered hawk in flight. Modified AI generated image.

Red-shouldered hawk perched. Modified from an istock photo.

GRAY HAWK
(Buteo plagiatus)

Size (Both Sexes): 18-19 in (46-48 cm), **Wingspan:** 3.3-3.6 ft (1-1.1 m)

Winter Range: Barely into Southern Arizona, southern New Mexico, and south Texas. Widespread in Mexico, Central America

Summer Range: Same as winter range, with some northern movement in breeding season

Diet: Small mammals, birds, lizards, and insects

Field Marks: This is a small and elegant Buteo. Adults are primarily gray with a finely barred tail and white underparts with fine gray barring. It's shape is Accipiter-like. The wings are short and broad, the tail relatively long, The legs are long and yellow.

Interesting Fact

Gray Hawks, with their short wings and long tail, are skilled at maneuvering through dense woodland. They often hunt by perching and waiting, or by flying slowly through their habitat.

Gray Hawk in flight. Note the Accipiter-like shape. Modified AI generated image.

Gray Hawk perched– modified AI generated image.

BUTEO-LIKE HAWKS

There are 3 species of medium to large-sized North American raptors, each in different genera, that look very much like Buteos, but are not classified in that genus. The White-tailed Hawk, Harris's Hawk, and Common Black Hawk.

WHITE-TAILED HAWK
(Geranoaetus albicaudatus)

Male Size: 17-22 in (43-56 cm), Wingspan: 48-54 in (1.2-1.4 m)

Female Size: 18-24 in (46-61 cm), Wingspan: 49-56 in(1.25-1.4 m)

Winter Range: Fairly common in its very limited US range- only coastal Texas grasslands, savannah and pastures. Also found in areas of Mexico, Central America, and South America

Summer Range: Same as winter range

Diet: Small mammals, birds, reptiles, and insects

Field Marks: Adults have a distinctive, almost bizarrely short, white tail with a broad black band, a pale gray body, dark flight feathers, and a reddish-brown shoulder patch. They have extremely wide wings. Juveniles have browner plumage with streaking on the underparts.

Interesting Facts

This species is known for its striking appearance and relatively small range within the United States. Long classified as a Buteo, genetic analysis has shown that it belongs in a different genus.

White-tailed hawk– modified AI generated image. Note the black tail band on pure white tail, and very broad wings.

HARRIS'S HAWK
(Parabuteo unicinctus)

Male Size: 18-22 in (46-56 cm), **Wingspan:** 41-47 in (104-119 cm)
Female Size: 20-25 in (51-64 cm), **Wingspan:** 46-50 in (117-127 cm)
Winter Range: Southwest United States, Mexico, Central and South America
Summer Range: Same as winter range
Diet: Small to medium-sized mammals like rabbits, birds, lizards
Field Marks- The adult is a dark chocolate-brown bird with rufous shoulders and prominent white tail band. In flight, all-dark wings with rufous wing linings. Juveniles are lighter in color with whitish toward wing tips. Also have white tail band. Harris's Hawks have long yellow legs.

Interesting Facts

They are known for their unique behavior of hunting cooperatively, in family groups. Harris's hawks are popular in falconry and relate well with humans. I have a close falconer friend who hunts almost exclusively with this species. They can be very aggressive, tenacious and capable hunters, taking game up to the size of adult jackrabbits.

Adult Harris Hawk in flight from an istock photo (kojihirano)

Modified AI-generated pair of Harris Hawks. Unique in their tendency to hunt as a family.

Immature captive Harris Hawk in flight. From a Pixabay photo (TheOtherKev)

COMMON BLACK HAWK
(Buteogallus anthracinus)

Male Size: 17-21 in (43-53 cm), **Wingspan: 48-50 in (122-127 cm)**
Female Size: 19-23 in (48-58 cm), **Wingspan:** 50-52 in (127–132 cm)
Winter Range: Mexico to South America
Summer Range: Riparian zones (near water) of the extreme southwestern United States (southern Arizona and Southwest NM) down to South America
Diet: Fish, reptiles, crayfish, fish, small mammals
Field marks– Extremely broad, black wings, and very short, fan-shaped tail with bold white band. Long yellow legs

Interesting Facts

They are more associated with riparian areas (near water) than most other North American raptors. They display some very particular behaviors– like wading in shallow water, and "herding" crayfish and fish into even shallower water in attempt to catch them.

Common Black Hawk in flight. AI did ok on this, but I had to make the wings wider and add a very short, white-banded tail.

Common Black Hawk- modified from a Pixabay photo (jkdvmim)

57

HARRIERS

Belonging to the genus Circus, harriers are medium-sized raptors known for their unique hunting style and distinct physical characteristics that set them apart from other birds of prey. Unlike robust Buteos, or agile falcons, harriers are slender, light birds with long tails and wings. They are adapted for low, slow flight over open terrain such as marshes, grasslands, and fields. They have a very owl-like facial disc and a flat face, which helps direct sound to their ears. Harriers often hunt by flying just a few feet off the ground, using their acute hearing and keen eyesight to detect small mammals, birds, and insects. There are numerous species of harrier worldwide, but we have only one species in North America, the Northern Harrier, formerly known as the Marsh Hawk.

NORTHERN HARRIER
(Circus hudsonius)

Body Size: Male: 18-19.7 inches (46-50 cm)   **Female:** 18.5-20.9 inches (47-53 cm)

Wingspan Male and Female: 40.2-46.5 inches (102-118 cm)

Summer Range: Breeds mainly in Canada and far northern parts of the United States.

Migration Range: Migrates through much of the United States.

Winter Range: Winters in southern United States, Mexico, and Central America.

Diet: Primarily small mammals and birds. Also feeds on amphibians, reptiles, and insects.

Field Marks: Long, narrow wings and long tail and white rump patch on top of tail base. It is its flight style that is so unusual- it is usually seen coursing slowly, low to the ground. Occasionally you will see one soaring or circling high up.

Male and female have very different coloration.

Male: Pale gray above, white below with black wingtips.

Female: Brown above, buff orangish streaks below, and barred tail.

Both Sexes: have the distinctive white rump patch and have the obvious round flat face and facial disk.

Interesting Facts

The Northern Harrier is unique among North American diurnal raptors for its owl-like facial disc- which helps it to hear rodents and other prey- as the bird is flying low over open fields and marshes. It hovers and flies very slowly and carefully, just feet off the ground, turning side to side, then plunges into the grass to nab its prey.

Adult male Northern Harrier-modified unsplash photo (Pete Nuij)

Classic almost white/silver male Northern Harrier. Modified from unsplash.com photo. (Pete Nuij)

Modified AI- generated Northern Harrier immature or female.

Female Northern Harrier – facial disc, long narrow wings and long tail. Modified from unsplash photo. (Pete Nuij)

KITES

Belonging to multiple genera and with many species found around the world, Kites are known for their graceful and buoyant flight. They have long, pointed wings and a relatively long tail, which contribute to their aerial agility, especially when hunting or soaring. Kites typically have a lighter build compared to hawks and eagles and are more adapted for feeding on smaller prey like insects, small mammals, and birds. Some species (like the Snail Kite and Hook-Billed Kite) specialize in very specific prey, in this case snails. In North America, there are 5 species in 5 different genera, so not very closely related to one another.

SNAIL KITE
(Rhostrhamus sociabilis)

Size (Both Sexes): 14-18 in **(36-45 cm), Wingspan:** 40-46 in (101-117 cm)
Winter Range: Florida, Central, and South America
Summer Range: Florida, parts of Central America
Diet: Almost exclusively apple snails
Field Marks- Broad wings with sharply curved, very narrow bill. Adult male is slate-gray. Adult female more mottled. Juveniles are brownish. Short square tail. white at the base.

Interesting Fact

Their sharply curved, narrow bill is specially adapted for extracting apple snails from their shells.

Smail Kite- modified from AI generated image.

HOOK-BILLED KITE
(Chondrohierax uncinatus)

Size (Both Sexes): 15-18 in (38-46 cm), **Wingspan:** 30-35 in (76-89 cm)

Winter Range: Very limited range in the United States. coastal southeast Texas, Mexico, Central, and South America

Summer Range: Same.

Diet: Snails, insects, small vertebrates

Field Marks- Extremely broad, short, heavily-barred, paddle-shaped, dark wings and long, broad, banded tail. A strangely shaped large bill, darker on top.

Interesting Fact

This strange-looking kite has a uniquely hooked bill for extracting snails from their shells, similar to the Snail Kite.

Hook-billed Kite in flight. Modified from AI generated image.

MISSISSIPPI KITE
(Ictinia mississippiensis)

Size (Both Sexes): 13-17 in **(33-43 cm)**, **Wingspan:** 30-37 in (76-94 cm)
Winter Range: South America
Summer Range: Central and southeastern United States.
Diet: Insects, small vertebrates
Field marks- A little smaller than a crow, with a flat gray color. Relatively long, pointed wings. Can be aggressive in defending their nest.

Interesting Facts

These kites are highly social and often seen in groups. They are agile fliers and feed mostly on the wing. I have seen this bird a few times in New Mexico, in the Rio Grande Valley. I was a bit shocked at this strange-looking bird in our area and it took me a while to identify it.

AI-generated image of a Mississippi Kite. A flat gray color, about the size of a crow.

Mississippi Kite in flight. Modified from unsplash photo.

WHITE-TAILED KITE
(Elanus leukurus)

Size (Both Sexes): 14-16 in (35-40 cm), **Wingspan:** 38-42 in (96-106 cm)
Winter Range: Western United States, Mexico
Summer Range: Western United States, Mexico, Central, and South America
Diet: Small mammals, particularly rodents
Field Marks- Slim, white bird with black "wrists" in flight. It is sometimes confused for gulls. When perched, you see the black shoulders on a white, slim bird.

Interesting Facts

These kites have a distinctive hovering flight while hunting. Once a threatened species, they have made a remarkable comeback due to conservation efforts. In the past, was called the Black-shouldered Kite, but name changed to White-tailed.

White-tailed Kite in flight. Modified from AI generated image.

White-tailed Kite perched- modified
from AI generated photo.

White-tailed Kite . Modified from
unsplash image (Y,S Santonii)

SWALLOW-TAILED KITE
(Elanoides forficatus)

Size (Both Sexes): 20-25 in (50-64 cm), **Wingspan**: 44-52 in (112-132 cm)
Winter Range: South America
Summer Range: Extreme southeastern United States over wetland forest.
Diet: Often snatch small lizards and snakes out of trees. They also eat insects, small mammals like mice, and small birds.
Field Marks- Hard to mistake for anything else. They have the black and white, sharply-contrasted plumage with deeply-forked, long tail. Long, pointed, narrow wings.

Interesting Facts

Known for their deeply-forked tail and striking black-and-white plumage, they are graceful fliers and usually take their prey in mid-air and do not land to eat. They eat on the wing. They also tend to skim water to drink during flight.

Swallow-tailed Kite in flight- hard to confuse with much else. Modified from AI generated image

ORDER: ACCIPTRIFORMES
FAMILY: PANDIONIDAE

THE OSPREY

Pandionidae, the sole member of which is the Osprey (Pandion haliaetus), is distinct from other Accipitridae due to evolutionary and ecological specialization. Ospreys have unique and specialized adaptations for feeding on fish, including reversible outer toes, and barbed pads on their feet for gripping slippery prey. Unlike typical Accipitridae members, Osprey life is centered around fish-containing water bodies. These distinct features justify the classification of Pandionidae as a separate family, reflecting the Osprey's evolutionary divergence and adaptation to a very specialized nichc.

OSPREY
(Pandion haliaetus)

Male Size: 21-23 in (53-58 cm), Wingspan: 5-6 ft (1.5-1.8 m)
Female Size: 22-25 in (56-64 cm), Wingspan: 5-6 ft (1.5-1.8 m)
Winter Range: South America, southern North America, coastal regions
Summer Range: All of North America, Europe, Asia, parts of Africa. Always near water.
Diet: Almost exclusively fish.
Field Marks: This is a large, white and dark raptor, almost always found near fish-containing water, Ospreys have long, narrow wings that noticeably bow downward when viewed from the front. They frequently hover over water before plunging in feet-first, up to about 3 feet deep. Their dark brown back contrasts with white head and underparts. A dark brown bar crosses the white of the head, through the eye. The beak is black and strongly curved.

They tend to make a bulky nest close to water in trees or on special nesting platforms.

Interesting Facts

Sometimes known as the "Fish Hawk," Ospreys are unique among North American raptors for their diet of live fish and their ability to plunge into the water to catch them. They have barbed pads on the soles of their feet to help grip slippery fish and specially adapted vision that allows them to see well through the glare and deep into the water. Their numbers were devastated by DDT, but since the DDT ban in the 1970's, they have made a remarkable comeback.

A great AI-generated image of an Osprey sitting on a stump by a lake.

I also really liked the AI generated Osprey in flight. Note the wings angling downward– a classic field mark.

NEW WORLD VULTURES

Vultures are large birds of prey, distinguished by eating almost exclusively carrion. They are essential scavengers in their ecosystems. They are divided into two families: the New World vultures of the Americas and the Old World vultures of Europe, Asia, and Africa. While those groups may look alike, Old and New World Vultures are actually not closely related at all.

Globally, there are 23 vulture species, with only 3 species residing in North America. Both Old and New World Vultures are highly adapted to consume dead animals, with highly acidic stomachs that neutralize bacteria and toxins, preventing disease spread. Their featherless heads are another adaptation for this lifestyle, reducing the problem of soiled head feathers from feeding deep inside large carcasses.

Many vulture species are solitary, but are social around carcasses and communal roosts. They tend to reproduce slowly, laying one to three eggs.

Vultures are vulnerable to population declines due to habitat loss, poisoning, and persecution. Populations of Old World vultures have plummeted in the last 30 years, with some species now critically endangered and most having only a fraction of their historic population. Fortunately, recent conservation efforts are slowing declines of some species.

Protecting these birds is vital for ecological balance and preventing the spread of diseases in both wildlife and human communities.

CALIFORNIA CONDOR
(Gynogyps californianus)

Size (Both Sexes): 43-55 in (109-140 cm), **Wingspan:** 9.5-10 ft (290-300 cm)

Winter Range: Scrubby, open country in Coastal California, the Grand Canyon of Arizona/ Utah , and northern Baja California in Mexico

Summer Range: Same as winter range.

Diet: Carrion, especially large mammals such as deer, cattle and smaller animals. Historically coastal populations ate beached whales and other marine animals. Condors locate carcasses with keen eyesight, and not by smell. They often follow other scavengers to a carcass.

Field Marks: It is the largest North American flying bird, far larger than any other bird of prey. It is sometimes confused for a small airplane! Adult has white fronts of wing. Younger birds are more solid dark, almost black. Adult has orange, bare head, while the young birds have more gray head.

Interesting Facts

The California Condor is still one of the world's rarest bird species. It was saved from the brink of extinction through intensive conservation efforts. The lowest population reached was 28 birds in the 1980s. There are now approximately 500 birds, with established populations in Arizona / Utah and Baja California. This massive effort has become a symbol of the potential for successful conservation programs.

A California Condor adult perched at the Grand Canyon. The body is about 4 feet long and the bird weighs about 30 pounds- extremely heavy for a flying bird. Modified AI image.

Adult California Condor in flight. Modified AI image. With a 10 foot wingspan, this bird can be confused for a small airplane!

TURKEY VULTURE
(Cathartes aura)

Male Size: 25-32 in (63-81 cm), **Wingspan:** 67-70 in (170-178 cm)
Female Size: 27-30 in (69-76 cm), **Wingspan:** 68-72 in (172-183 cm)
Winter Range: Very southern United States to South America
Summer Range: Widespread and common throughout North America
Diet: Carrion. Unlike most raptors, they have a highly developed sense of smell to help them find it.
Field Marks- Turkey Vultures are common across the country during the warm months, and are often seen roosting and soaring in groups. Rocking flight is a good way to tell them from eagles and hawks at long distances. Their long wings form a shallow "V" when viewing them from the front, called a dihedral. Soaring birds dip (drop) their wings periodically, which is a pattern of flight unique to them. They have a small, red, featherless head. They have "two-tone" wings- silvery flight feathers in contrast to dark front of wing.

Interesting Fact

Known in Mexico and south as "Sopilotes" meaning "so-so pilots". This relates to their rocking, almost drunken- appearing soaring.

Turkey Vulture adult from an Unsplash image (J. Cotten)

Turkey Vulture adult, note the two-tone wings. Image modified from unsplash photo (Shlomo Shalev)

BLACK VULTURE
(Coragyps atratus)

Size (Both Sexes): 22-29 in (56-74 cm), **Wingspan:** 4.6-5.3 ft (1.4-1.6 m)

Winter Range: Southeastern United States to South America

Summer Range: Southeastern United States, extending into the Midwest and Northeast during summer

Diet: Carrion, occasionally eggs, and newborn or weak animals.

Field Marks: More flapping flight than Turkey Vulture, less soaring. Very broad wings are relatively flat when viewed from front unlike the Turkey Vulture. Wings have silvery patches at tips. Small black, naked head with narrow beak. Short tail.

Interesting Fact

Black Vultures often feed in groups and are known to follow Turkey Vultures to carcasses, as they have a less developed sense of smell.

A Common Black Vulture perched on a stump. A modified AI image.

Common Black Vulture in flight. Note the short tail and very broad, fairly short wings with white tips, and the small black head. Modified AI image.

ORDER: FALCONIFORMES
FAMILY:FALCONIDAE

THE FALCONS AND CARACARAS

The order Falconiformes, primarily comprising falcons and caracaras, is characterized by several distinct features. Unlike Accipitriformes, Falconiformes have a tooth-like notch on their beaks, which can aid in killing prey. Acciptriformes tend to use their powerful feet for that purpose. As a group, the falcons are generally smaller, more dense, and more aerodynamically built compared to Accipitriformes.

In the past, because of similar predatory behavior, biologists assumed that falcons and hawks had to be relatively closely related. This turns out not to be the case. Recent genetic analysis shows falcons and caracaras to be more closely related to parrots and songbirds than they are to hawks and other raptors!

Caracaras are very different-seeming from falcons, and it seems odd that they are closely related. Many of the caracara species are opportunistic scavengers and predators of small prey.

CARACARAS

Caracaras are found in the New World (North, Central and South America) and are grouped with falcons primarily because of their similar notched beak structure. Genetic analysis shows their close relationship with falcons, despite their very different appearance and lifestyles. There are about 20 species of Caracara worldwide, all in the Americas, but only one species lives here in North America. The Common (Crested) Caracara is a regular inhabitant of our southern States. The other species live further south, from Mexico to the tip of Tierra del Fuego in Patagonia and on surrounding islands.

COMMON CARACARA
CRESTED CARACARA
(Caracara cheriway)

Size (Both Sexes): 19-23 in (48-58 cm), **Wingspan:** 4-4.5 ft (1.2-1.4 m)

Winter Range: Southern United States, Mexico, Central and South America

Summer Range: Southern United States, particularly in Texas, Florida, and Arizona; also in Mexico, Central and South America

Diet: Carrion, small animals, insects, and occasionally birds and reptiles

Field Marks– Often stands on or near the ground. It stands out with its distinctive appearance, with a black cap, white neck, and large beak with red facial skin. When flying, it has black wings with bold white patches near the wingtips. Seen from front or behind, it has a downward slope to its wings

Interesting Facts

The Common Caracara is both a scavenger and predator, often seen walking on the ground. It is surprising that caracaras are actually members of the falcon family. Some caracara species are known for their boldness, often taking food from other birds, and even from people.

An adult Common or Crested Caracara- modified AI generated image.

FALCONS

Family: Falconidae: Genus Falco

FALCONS- Known as "long-wings" by falconers, all have distinctive narrow, angled and pointed wings. They have compact, solid but streamlined bodies and long tails. This dense, aerodynamic build enables rapid flight and exceptionally high-speed dives (called stoops). Many are specialists in taking birds out of the air. When in the stoop, the Peregrine Falcon is the fastest animal on the planet- clocked at well over 200 mph.

There are about 40 species of falcons worldwide, of a few different genera, scattered across every continent except Antarctica, In North America, we have only 6 species, and they are all in the genus Falco. They range from the tiny, common and colorful American Kestrel, to the very large and magnificent Gyrfalcon. I organize them here by size, starting with the smallest.

AMERICAN KESTREL
(Falco sparverius)

Male Size: 8.7-12 in (22-30 cm), **Wingspan:** 20-24 in (51-61 cm)
Female Size: 9.4-12 in (24-30 cm), **Wingspan:** 22-25 in (56-64 cm)
Winter Range: Relatively common throughout North and South America
Summer Range: Throughout North America
Diet: Insects, small mammals, small birds mostly sparrow-sized.
Field Marks-The males are very colorful with prominent black mask, a rich rust-colored back and slate-blue shoulders, while the females have more subdued colors. They are smaller than a robin, slim and delicate but with a relatively large head. They have the typical falcon shape, with narrow, pointed wings. Unlike most falcons though, American Kestrels frequently hover when hunting, beating the wings rapidly.

Interesting Facts

Sometimes (incorrectly) called Sparrow Hawk, the American Kestrel is the smallest and most colorful falcon in North America. This was the first bird I rehabilitated as a child. They remain a favorite of mine.

Photos my son took of Kestrels at our next box behind our house near Santa Fe, NM

The coloring of the adult male American Kestrel- our most brightly colored raptor! Modified AI-generated image looks a little strange to me, but the colors and general shape are generally accurate.

The coloring of the female American Kestrel- modified AI generated image.

MERLIN
(PIGEON HAWK)
(Falco columbarius)

Male Size: 9.4-11.8 in (24-30 cm), **Wingspan:** 20.9-26.8 in (53-68 cm)

Female Size: 10.2-12.6 in (26-32 cm), **Wingspan:** 23.6-29.5 in (60-75 cm)

Winter Range: Southern Canada, all of the United States, northern Mexico

Summer Range: Northern United States, especially Pacific Northwest, Canada, Alaska

Diet: Small birds up to the size of waxwings and horned larks, large insects. They don't stoop as Peregrines do, but usually chase their prey down and catch them in mid-air.

Field Marks: Usually a relatively dark-colored bird, with classic small falcon shape. There are multiple different populations with different markings. Adult males tend to have bluish back and streaked breast. Females have brown back. Most color morphs have a black and white banded tail. Typical falcon shape-narrow pointed wings and narrow relatively long tail. They are much smaller than Peregrine and Prairie Falcons but larger than American Kestrel. Heavier-looking than American Kestrel, and a more powerful, more direct flier.

Interesting Facts

Also known as the Pigeon Hawk, Merlins have great color variation, with some populations very dark and others very light. It makes identification difficult. You must rely on shape, size and appropriate location at appropriate times of year.

This is based on a photo I took years ago of a young Merlin perched on the fist of my falconer friend, Michael Melloy.

Merlin in flight. Note the black and white banded tail. Modified from istock photo (Brian E Kushner)

APLOMADO FALCON
(Falco femoralis)

Male Size: 12-16 in (30-41 cm), **Wingspan:** 29-32 in (74-81 cm)
Female Size: 14-17 in (36-43 cm), **Wingspan:** 31-34 in (79-86 cm)
Winter Range: Southern United States, Gulf Coast, Mexico, Central and South America
Summer Range: Southern New Mexico, South Texas, very limited range in United States, more into Mexico
Diet: Birds, large insects, small mammals
Field Marks- A lightly-built, narrow-winged falcon with a very long, banded tail. Thin white rim to back of wing in contrast to dark rest of wing. Adult coloring: White and black mask, breast is white above, with a dark band and buff orange abdomen. Juvenile has darker breast. Aplomado is more slim, and more lightly built than Peregrine or Prairie, and it is obviously larger than a Kestrel or Merlin.

Interesting Facts

They were more common in far south Texas, New Mexico and Arizona 100 years ago, but are now very rare. They are being reintroduced in parts of Texas. Aplomado Falcons are known for their cooperative hunting strategy, often hunting in pairs or groups.

Modified AI images of Aplomado Falcon perched and in flight.

PRAIRIE FALCON
(Falco mexicanus)

Male Size: 14.6-16.5 in (37-42 cm), **Wingspan:** 35-40 in (89-102 cm)
Female Size: 16.5-18.1 in (42-46 cm), **Wingspan:** 40-44 in (102-112 cm)
Winter Range: Western and central United States
Summer Range: Same as winter, extends into Canada
Diet: Small mammals- ground squirrels in particular, birds up to the size of ducks, but often smaller birds.
Field Marks: Wings a little less pointed than Peregrine. Wing beats appear stiffer and shorter. In general it is a much lighter-colored bird than the Peregrine. Usually a pale brown back with whitish streaked breast. They have dark "armpits" or axilla in flight.

Interesting Fact

This falcon prefers open, arid country. It is often seen hunting at high speeds over prairies, chapparal and deserts of the western US.

A modified AI-generated Prairie Falcon- showing the relatively light- colored back.

A modified AI-generated Prairie Falcon looks over its desert canyon domain.

A modified AI-generated Prairie Falcon in flight.

PEREGRINE FALCON
(Falco peregrinus)

Male Size: 14-19 in (36-48 cm), **Wingspan:** 31-40 in (79-102 cm)
Female Size: 16-20 in (41-51 cm), **Wingspan:** 41-46 in (105-117 cm)
Winter Range: Worldwide
Summer Range: Worldwide
Diet: Birds up to the size of large ducks, bats
Field Marks: Adults have slate-blue dark back, lighter front with obvious black or dark mask. Juveniles are more brown, with less developed mask. Fast and powerful in direct flight with pointed wings. Seems heavier and more powerful in flight, and much darker than Prairie Falcon, its closest relative in the US. It is much larger than Merlin or Kestrel, and heavier and larger than Aplomado Falcon.

Interesting Fact

The fastest animal on the planet, capable of diving at over 200 mph. It uses this terrific dive (called a stoop) to knock birds- up to the size of large ducks- out of the sky. The Peregrine is possibly the most highly regarded falconry bird of all.

Peregrine in flight. Modified from an unsplash photo (Mathew Schwartz)

AI generated Peregrine adult.

GYRFALCON
(Falco rusticolus)

Male Size: 14-19 in (36-48 cm), Wingspan: 31-40 in (79-102 cm)
Male Size: 20-24 in (51-61 cm), Wingspan: 47-63 in (120-160 cm)
Female Size: 22-25 in (56-64 cm), Wingspan: 51-65 in (130-165 cm)
Winter Range: Northern United States, southern Canada
Summer Range: Arctic regions including Alaska, northern Canada, Greenland, and parts of Eurasia
Diet: Birds (especially Ptarmigan, ducks), small mammals
Field marks- A very large, powerful falcon, noticeably larger than Prairie or Peregrine. Different subspecies have different colors. The Arctic Gyrfalcon is white, while other subspecies are dark grayish. The juveniles tend to be brownish and streaked.

Interesting Facts

The Gyrfalcon is the largest of the falcon species worldwide, and has a variety of plumage colorations, from nearly pure white to dark gray. It is known for its large size, powerful build and endurance. It's highly regarded in falconry due to its size, strength, and beauty.

Gyrfalcon in flight. Modified from photo from observation.org

A cold-looking scene of a Gyrfalcon on a rocky tower in the Arctic. AI generated.

A FINAL WORD...

I hope that this little handbook has given you a glimpse into the fascinating world of North American Raptors. Spend some time observing these birds, and I would be surprised if you didn't become enchanted by them as I did so many years ago. They are noble and beautiful. If you learn to appreciate them, perhaps you will be moved to join the effort to conserve them. Be sure to look for the companion volume to this book **"Raptors of North America- A Coloring Book of North American Birds of Prey"** In the final pages of this book, I provide some reference resources for raptor identification and biology, some important raptor conservation organizations, and some resources on lead toxicity in raptors.

Did you know there's a creative way to further engage with the world of raptors detailed in this book?

Complement your journey through "An Introduction to North American Birds of Prey" with our accompanying **"A Coloring Book of North American Birds of Prey."** This coloring book serves as a perfect artistic extension, allowing you to immerse yourself visually and creatively with the birds you've learned about.

Perfect for enthusiasts of all ages, this coloring book is a wonderful tool to solidify your knowledge and appreciation of North American birds of prey. Pick up your copy today and color your way through the fascinating world of raptors!

REFERENCES

Sibley, D. A. (2014). **The Sibley Guide to Birds, second edition.** Alfred A. Knopf, New York, NY, USA.

Wikipedia- various articles.

All About Birds Website (Cornell University) https://AllAboutBirds.org

LINKS AND RESOURCES ON LEAD POISONING IN RAPTORS

Link to an article I wrote about Lead Poisoning and Golden Eagles https://horsesidevetguide.com/Save+Golden+Eagles+with+Lead+Free+Bullets

Hunting with non-lead - an excellent, balanced resource created by hunters and wildlife biologists. https://huntingwithnonlead.org

The Peregrine Fund – Lead Poisoning in Raptors

Website: https://www.peregrinefund.org/lead-poisoning-raptors

Summary: The Peregrine Fund provides detailed information on lead poisoning in raptors, including its causes, effects, and methods for prevention. This resource also offers insights into ongoing research and conservation efforts to mitigate the impacts of lead poisoning.

Raptor Research Foundation – Lead Poisoning

Website: https://www.raptorresearchfoundation.org/lead-poisoning

Summary: The Raptor Research Foundation offers valuable resources on lead poisoning in raptors, including scientific articles, conference proceedings, and educational materials aimed at increasing awareness and understanding of this issue among researchers, conservationists, and the general public.

BirdLife International – Lead Poisoning in Birds

Website:

https://www.birdlife.org/worldwide/programmes/preventing-poisoning-birds

Summary: BirdLife International's Preventing Poisoning in Birds program addresses various sources of poisoning, including lead, and provides resources and guidelines for preventing and mitigating the impacts of lead poisoning on bird populations, including raptors.

U.S. Fish and Wildlife Service - Lead Poisoning in Birds of Prey

Website: https://www.fws.gov/birds/solve/lead-poisoning-in-birds-of-prey.php

Summary: The U.S. Fish and Wildlife Service offers information on lead poisoning specifically in birds of prey, highlighting the risks posed by lead ammunition and fishing tackle, as well as efforts to address this issue through policy, research, and outreach.

American Bird Conservancy - Lead Poisoning

Website: https://abcbirds.org/issue/lead-poisoning/

Summary: The American Bird Conservancy provides resources and advocacy efforts aimed at reducing lead poisoning in birds, including raptors, by promoting alternatives to lead ammunition and tackling other sources of lead contamination in the environment.

RESOURCES ON RAPTORS
AND THEIR IDENTIFICATION

All About Birds: by Cornell Lab of Ornithology
Website: https://www.allaboutbirds.org
Summary: All About Birds offers comprehensive information on North American bird species, including detailed descriptions, range maps, photos, and audio recordings, making it an invaluable resource for raptor identification.

The Audubon Guide to North American Birds
Website: https://www.audubon.org/bird-guide
Summary: With an extensive database of bird species, including raptors, Audubon's guide provides detailed profiles, range maps, and multimedia resources to aid in bird identification and conservation efforts.

eBird : by Cornell Lab of Ornithology
Website: https://ebird.org/home
Summary: eBird allows users to explore bird sightings, including raptors, submitted by a global community of birders, providing invaluable data for identification, distribution, and conservation research.

Merlin Bird ID by Cornell Lab of Ornithology
Website: https://merlin.allaboutbirds.org
Summary: Merlin Bird ID offers an intuitive tool for identifying birds, including raptors, based on user-provided information such as location, size, and color, supplemented by expertly curated photo galleries and audio recordings.

HawkWatch International's Hawk ID
Website: https://hawkwatch.org/hawkwatch-id
Summary: HawkWatch International's Hawk ID provides resources specifically made for identifying North American hawks, eagles, falcons, and other raptors, including species profiles, photos, and migration information.

ORGANIZATIONS INVOLVED IN RAPTOR PRESERVATION WORLDWIDE

The Peregrine Fund
Website: https://www.peregrinefund.org
Summary: Globally renowned for its efforts in conserving raptors, The Peregrine Fund conducts research, habitat restoration, and educational programs aimed at safeguarding various species.

BirdLife International
Website: https://www.birdlife.org
Summary: BirdLife International works across continents to protect raptors and their habitats through policy advocacy, community engagement, and conservation projects.

HawkWatch International
Website: https://hawkwatch.org
Summary: Focused on monitoring and protecting raptor populations during migration, HawkWatch International conducts research, public outreach, and habitat conservation efforts.

The Raptor Research Foundation
Website: https://www.raptorresearchfoundation.org
Summary: Dedicated to advancing scientific understanding and conservation of raptors, The Raptor Research Foundation supports research initiatives, conferences, and educational outreach programs worldwide.

The Hawk Conservancy Trust
Website: https://www.hawk-conservancy.org
Summary: Based in the UK, The Hawk Conservancy Trust focuses on conservation breeding, rehabilitation, and public education to raise awareness about raptor conservation.

The National Audubon Society

Website: https://www.audubon.org

Summary: With a wide-ranging conservation mission, The National Audubon Society plays a significant role in protecting raptor habitats and advocating for policies that benefit birds of prey.

The World Center for Birds of Prey

Website: https://www.peregrinefund.org/world-center

Summary: Operated by The Peregrine Fund, the World Center for Birds of Prey serves as a hub for research, breeding programs, and public education on raptor conservation.

The Raptor Trust

Website: https://theraptortrust.org

Summary: Providing critical care to injured and orphaned raptors, The Raptor Trust also delivers educational programs to promote awareness and appreciation for these birds.

The International Association for Falconry&Conservation of Birds of Prey

Website: https://www.iaf.org

Summary: Supporting sustainable falconry practices and conservation efforts, this association collaborates with experts and enthusiasts globally to protect raptor species and their habitats.

The Raptors Trust

Website: https://theraptorstrust.org

Summary: Operating in India, The Raptors Trust focuses on conservation research, habitat restoration, and community engagement to protect endangered raptors and their ecosystems.

Hawks Aloft, Inc.

Website: https://hawksaloft.org

Summary: A non-profit organization started in 1994 and based in Albuquerque, New Mexico. They work to conserve indigenous wild birds and their habitats through avian research, conservation education, raptor rescue, and cooperation with other organizations.

Made in United States
Troutdale, OR
12/02/2024

25701759R00069